SIX DANCERS OF SADLER'S WELLS

Julia Farron in *Façade*   (*Anthony*)

DANCERS OF TO-DAY NO. 10

JULIA FARRON

The Puritan Hannah in *A Mirror for Witches*

" Over many years a portrait gallery rich in characterisation and colour "

DANCERS OF TO-DAY NO. 10

SIX
DANCERS OF SADLER'S WELLS

JULIA FARRON   LESLIE EDWARDS   ROSEMARY LINDSAY

ALEXANDER GRANT   ELAINE FIFIELD   DAVID BLAIR

by

CYRIL SWINSON

LONDON
ADAM AND CHARLES BLACK

FIRST PUBLISHED 1956

A. & C. BLACK LIMITED
4, 5 & 6 SOHO SQUARE
LONDON, W.1

CONTENTS

INTRODUCTION

The ballerinas of a Company inevitably attract most of the limelight, but it is true to say that the all-round excellence of a Company is dependent to a great extent on the supporting dancers : the *premier danseurs* the soloists and the *corps de ballet*.

This book is devoted to six dancers, all of whom are contributing to-day to the all-round excellence of the Sadler's Wells Ballet—Julia Farron and Leslie Edwards, who have both been with the Company for more than twenty years, Rosemary Lindsay and Alexander Grant, who have made their reputations more recently with the Company, and Elaine Fifield and David Blair, two young dancers who may well become two of the outstanding dancers of the Sadler's Wells Ballet in the coming years.

MADE IN GREAT BRITAIN

PRINTED BY MORRISON AND GIBB LIMITED, LONDON AND EDINBURGH

CARNAVAL: Julia Farron and Leslie Edwards

JULIA FARRON

" WHAT would the Company do without Miss Farron ? " *The Times* once enquired when reviewing a performance in which she had danced quite different types of parts in all three of the ballets performed.

The ballerina rôles in the great classical ballets have eluded her, but every other type of part has come her way : Miss Farron is indeed one of the most versatile and intelligent dancers in ballet to-day, excelling in *demi-caractère* and character rôles.

Born on 22nd July 1922, she began dancing at an early age. She was a successful pupil at the Cone School and gained many academic honours. In 1934, at the age of twelve and a half, she was a " child solo dancer " in the Christmas pantomime at Drury Lane Theatre, and in 1935, Will o' the Wisp in a popular children's play, *Bluebell in Fairyland.* Earlier in 1935 she had appeared with a fellow pupil at a Cone School display in a scene called " The Picture." " Joyce Farron-Smith," said one reviewer, " is a very promising young dancer," adding that her companion, Glynis Johns, " was very good as the Dancing Master."

It was also in 1935 that she was awarded a Junior Scholarship at Sadler's Wells. Her first student appearance with the Company was on 22nd October 1935, when she was the child Clara in *Casse-Noisette.* In the following Christmas

holidays she took part in a special student performance of *Nursery Suite*, appearing as Bo-Peep.

In 1936 she became a full member of the Company, and her first created rôle was in *A Wedding Bouquet.* She was Pepé, the dog, and her performance delighted everyone. She made steady progress in the Company, dancing in the *corps de ballet* and appearing in most of the new ballets. She was a Red Pawn in *Checkmate*, in the *pas de quatre* in *Les Rendez-vous* and a page in *Le Roi Nu.* She also danced Columbine in *Carnaval*, although she was not really ready for it. In the production of *The Sleeping Princess* in 1939 she danced the Breadcrumb Fairy in the Prologue, in which she was, in the words of an eminent critic, " exceedingly brilliant." Her first big opportunity came in April 1939, when Ashton created for her the part of Psyche in *Cupid and Psyche* (music by Lord Berners). Ashton used her soft and fluid style beautifully, and her dances were the best part of what proved to be a disappointing ballet. It was withdrawn after only three performances, and to the young dancers in it—Frank Staff, Michael Somes and Julia Farron —it was a painful disappointment.

There was another disappointment which Miss Farron had to face. In physique she was growing away from the perfect proportions of the purely classical dancer. In her early years at the Wells,

NURSERY SUITE : Jack and Jill and Little Bo-Peep.
Jill Gregory, Mollie Brown and Julia Farron

Anthony

it had seemed probable that she would become an out-standing classical dancer. Her performances had shown great promise : they were elegant and full of interest, but too mannered possibly to be truly classical : " startled nymph " performances Arnold Haskell once called them. Her ability to express character in her dancing, which was to prove such an asset in later years, was a disadvantage when her ambition was to be a classical dancer.

These setbacks in Miss Farron's career came when she was still in her teens. Dancers with less fortitude and intelligence would have resigned themselves to the *corps de ballet* or sought employment elsewhere. Miss Farron became instead a *demi-caractère* dancer, specialising in those rôles in

A WEDDING BOUQUET :
Margot Fonteyn : Julia, Julia Farron : Her Dog Pepé

Anthony

which characterisation and interpretation are as essential parts of the rôle as technique. As Estrella, she captured the true flavour of *Carnaval*, showing a sense of style which eludes most English dancers, and as Mlle. Theodore in *The Prospect Before Us*, a part in which she succeeded Pamela May, she gave a delightful and animated performance. From the sophistication of Mlle. Theodore, she passed easily to the rustic milkmaid in *Façade*. There were other ballets in the war years in which she gave notable performances : in *The Gods Go A-Begging*, in *The Haunted Ballroom*, as Faith in Ashton's *The Quest*, as Dawn in *Coppélia*, and as a blue girl and then a red girl in *Les Patineurs*. As one of the white skaters in this ballet she had a sparkle and style which few of her successors have achieved.

When the Company moved to the Royal Opera House in 1946 Miss Farron was the Queen in *The Sleeping Beauty*. She was perhaps too young for the part, but she looked enchanting and moved with regal style and grace. To wile away the tedious hours of her hundred years' sleep between Act I and Act III, she was also one of the Duchesses in Act II. She reigned as queen for countless performances in the early years at Covent Garden. She was also Princess Bathilde in *Giselle*, making her a real character and not merely a piece of well-dressed pasteboard. " Miss Farron is the finest Bathilde I have ever seen," Peter Williams, the editor of *Dance and Dancers*, declared in 1952, a view which is endorsed by many who have seen countless performances of the ballet. Another outstanding part was as the Prostitute in *Miracle in the Gorbals*, which she took over from Celia Franca. She endowed it with a sultry sensuousness that made it completely realistic, but within the framework of ballet. Her sudden conversion by the Stranger was beautifully done and entirely convincing.

In a revival of *Checkmate* in 1947 Miss Farron was the Red Queen, and was notable in it for the tenderness and sincerity she displayed. Although she danced other rôles—the Wardrobe Mistress in Helpmann's short-lived *Adam Zero*, a Child of Light in *Dante Sonata*, the Tarantella in *La Boutique Fantasque* (with Harold Turner), Violet in *A Wedding Bouquet*, the Lady Belerma in *Don Quixote*, her frequent performances as the Queen in *The Sleeping Beauty* seemed to suggest that her best dancing days were over, and that she was resigned for ever to non-dancing rôles such as these.

It was wrong to contemplate such a thing, for in 1950 she appeared in the *corps de ballet* of *Ballet Imperial*, " where the crisp, clean quality of her dancing," as John Percival described it, set an excellent example to her colleagues. But the accumulated effect of her performances of Queens and Princesses, tended to over-shadow her other work, until during the season 1950–51 she danced the ballerina rôle in *Ballet Imperial*. It was a part not obviously suited to her, and at first she

THE SLEEPING PRINCESS :
The Sapphire Fairy

THE HAUNTED BALLROOM : Alicia
All photographs on this page by Anthony

CUPID AND PSYCHE : Psyche

lacked the authority the part demanded, but she quickly gained assurance, and her vigour and speed in the third movement of the ballet especially were outstanding.

Since that season Miss Farron has begun a new era of accomplishment and achievement. In Ashton's *Daphnis and Chloé*, she was one of the three Nymphs of Pan, and later the seductive and alluring Lykanion. A few months later, she created the part of the King's Guest in Massine's *Donald of the Burthens*. It was a small part, but with intelligence and understanding she made it a sympathetic and convincing character. A greater opportunity came with her next new part. Hannah, in Andrée Howard's ballet *A Mirror for Witches*, was a Puritan wife, hard, narrow-minded and jealous. Although there was little obvious detail in it, she built up a strong, unforgiving and unforgettable character. By just the right attitude of head and body, with few but significant movements of her hands, she established the character of this bitter, warped woman.

THE SLEEPING PRINCESS :
The Breadcrumb Fairy

CARNAVAL : Columbine

IN *THE LORD OF BURLEIGH*

A tiny cameo as a theatrical neighbour in *Bonne Bouche* came next, followed by the Goddess Diana in Ashton's full-length ballet *Sylvia*. Here again the part was small and she did not appear until the third act, but in a few seconds she established the part and was magnificent in her rage against the enemies of Sylvia.

In the new production of *Le Lac des Cygnes* in 1952, Ashton created for Act III a Neapolitan Dance for two dancers. It has great speed and *joie de vivre*, and on the first night and on every occasion since when they have danced it, Julia Farron and Alexander Grant make it one of the most exhilarating moments of the evening. She often appears also as one of the four leading swans, and on many other occasions she has been the Princess-Mother.

Her next new part was in Frederick Ashton's short ballet *Rinaldo and Armida*. In this work which was virtually a *pas de deux* for Somes and Beriosova, as Sybilla the Sorceress the little she had to do was a distinctive contribution to the eerie atmosphere of this strange and lovely work.

The performance in 1956 to celebrate the tenth anniversary of the re-opening of the Royal Opera House was *The Sleeping Beauty*. Miss Farron was no longer on the throne, and she appeared as one of Florestan's two Sisters, dancing with such spirit and gaiety that the part seemed to gain new brilliance. In later performances she danced The Fairy of the Enchanted Garden with great finish and charm, and perfect timing.

LES RENDEZ-VOUS: In the *Pas de Quatre*

CUPID AND PSYCHE: Psyche

Miss Farron dances many other parts in the repertoire, and gives much more than competent performances in rôles for which she is not ideally suited. In *Les Sylphides* she dances the Valse, and on occasion, the Prelude, in both of which she is excellent. She is admirable as one of the leading Wilis in *Giselle*, and one longs to see her as the Queen: it seems to be a part made for her.

In *Mam'zelle Angot* as the Aristocrat she is not happily cast, and only perhaps Shearer and Pamela May have been entirely successful in the long *pas de deux* with the Caricaturist in the second scene. Of all her parts perhaps the two most lovely and rewarding are her Betrayed Girl, and as one of Job's daughters. In *Job* she has a sweet sensitivity and grace that appear with new freshness and beauty on the rare occasions that *Job* is performed. In *The Rake's Progress* her Betrayed Girl has a poignant beauty and humility that are most moving. She danced this rôle at the twenty-fifth anniversary performance of the Sadler's Wells Ballet. It was a worthy tribute to her, not only for the fact that she is an outstanding *demi-caractère* dancer in the Company but for the long years of service she has given to it, and will give, it is hoped, in the years to come.

All photographs on these two pages by Anthony,
except Hamlet: The Queen, which is by Baron.

THE RAKE'S PROGRESS: The Betrayed Girl   *MIRACLE IN THE GORBALS:*   The Prostitute

HAMLET: The Queen   *THE PROSPECT BEFORE US:* Mademoiselle Theodore

Roger Wood
DAPHNIS AND CHLOÉ: Lykanion

John Hart
LE LAC DES CYGNES: In the Tarantella

Anthony
THE SLEEPING BEAUTY: One of Florestan's Sisters

Anthony
CHECKMATE: The Red Queen

THE SLEEPING BEAUTY : Leslie Edwards as Cattalabutte, Julia Farron as the Queen, David Davenport as King Florestan

LESLIE EDWARDS

HIS long career as a dancer has rarely earned him more than a mention in the critics' reports, but to the audiences who have seen him through the years at the Sadler's Wells Theatre, at the New Theatre and at Covent Garden, he has a special place in their affections and admiration. They remember the rise of the curtain in *The Sleeping Beauty*, when with magnificent assurance and dignity he summons the courtiers to attend the christening of the Princess. They remember him as Hilarion in *Giselle*, jealous and foreboding, as Benno, the Prince's friend, in *Le Lac des Cygnes*, and in a variety of other parts which he has made especially his own.

He has a fine sense of theatre, and although he must have played Cattalabutte in *The Sleeping Beauty* hundreds of times, every performance has the same freshness of approach, the same concentration, and the same attention to detail.

Like other senior members of the Company, Mr. Edwards is now devoting more time to teaching, after a successful début in this rôle at a summer school in Canada in 1954. Another task for which he is eminently well qualified would be to lecture on the history of the Company, of which he has been a member since 1933.

Leslie Edwards was born at Teddington, Middlesex, in 1916. He was a pupil of Madame Bromova, an excellent teacher, who encouraged

him in his ambition to become an actor or a dancer. When he left school at fifteen he found it difficult to find employment on the stage, and a sympathetic aunt encouraged him to go to Madame Rambert. She accepted him as a pupil, and it was not long before he began to appear in ballet performances at the little Mercury Theatre. Towards the end of 1932 Miss de Valois required an extra boy for a revival of Rupert Doone's *The Enchanted Grove*, and young Edwards was sent along to Sadler's Wells Theatre. He started rehearsing in December 1932, and made his first appearance with the Company in January 1933. He became a permanent member during the season of 1933–34, and apart from his war service, he has been with the Company ever since.

Leslie Edwards soon found himself appearing in most of the works in the repertoire, in the *corps de ballet*, and occasionally in small parts. In the new production of *Casse-Noisette* in 1937 he was one of the three boys dancing the *Danse Arabe*. He was in the *pas de huit* in *Les Patineurs* in 1937, and the same year he created the part of Arthur in Ashton's *A Wedding Bouquet*. (He played the same part twelve years later when the ballet was revived at the Royal Opera House.) In the seasons of 1937–39 he was a Red Castle in *Checkmate*, in the *pas de six* in *Les Rendez-vous*, a Guard in *Le Roi Nu* and the Camellia Fairy's

GISELLE : Hilarion

Anthony

Leslie Hurry, he was Benno, with Robert Helpmann as the Prince and Margot Fonteyn as Odette–Odile. Benno is a small part, but well-played it can make an important contribution to the Prince's performance. " It would be difficult to find a better Benno as portrayed by Leslie Edwards," Cyril Beaumont has written, " who looks a gentleman and whose stage manners are impeccable, always friendly, courtly and gracious, but never presuming on the Prince's friendship." In 1944 he danced again his old part of Florestan in *Carnaval* and created the Beggar in *Miracle in the Gorbals*. It was a perfect little cameo, and revealed once more how excellent an actor he was.

When the Sadler's Wells Ballet moved to the Royal Opera House in 1946, opening with *The Sleeping Beauty*, Edwards was Cattalabutte, and he has always played this part except on the few occasions when he has danced the Wicked Fairy. He makes an excellent Carabosse, but the ballet never seems quite the same if he is not there as Cattalabutte to direct the opening ceremonies. (In the pre-war production of the ballet he was, on occasion, a most regal and dignified King Florestan.)

When *The Rake's Progress* was revived at Covent Garden, he was the Hornblower, and at different times he has danced other parts in the ballet. I like especially to see him as The Bravo, a sinister, lecherous character in his hands. He has also danced the Rake, and his success in the part, and in the title rôle of *Don Quixote* which he took over at a few hours' notice, makes one regret that more leading parts have not come his way.

In Helpmann's spectacular *Adam Zero*, he was the Mime (Adam Zero's Spiritual adviser), the Ghost in Helpmann's *Hamlet* when it was revived in 1946, and in Ashton's lavish but unsuccessful Edwardian ballet, *Les Sirènes*, he was a dashing chauffeur to Fonteyn's glamorous La Bolero. His next notable creation was as The Butcher in *Mam'zelle Angot*, a tiny part but a gem of characterisation. He was the Insect King in Massine's *Clock Symphony*, the Hairdresser in Ashton's *Cinderella*, a Priest in *Don Quixote*, and in fact in most of the new ballets of this period there seemed to be a character part for him, which he took in his stride. Then in 1951–52 he had a succession of more important rôles. As

Cavalier in *The Sleeping Princess*. He was a Child of Light in *Dante Sonata* in 1940, and in a new production of *Coppélia* in April 1940 he was the Duke. Later the same year he was one of the three comic lawyers in *The Prospect Before Us*, with Michael Somes and Richard Ellis.

A new production of *Façade* was mounted in 1940, and although Mr. Edwards was not in the first cast, he danced in it shortly afterwards, and he has danced all the male parts in the ballet. On one occasion at the New Theatre, when he was one of the three mountaineers in the Yodelling Song, his two companions missed their entrance, and Edwards danced alone with the milkmaid, and somehow provided all the essential parts of the cow, which are normally shared between the three boys. He was in the Services for two years, but was invalided out in 1943. On his return, in Ashton's ballet *The Quest*, he created the part of Archimago, a magician personifying hypocrisy. On 7th September 1943, in a new production of *Le Lac des Cygnes*, with scenery and costumes by

Felix Fonteyn

A WEDDING BOUQUET: Leslie Edwards as Arthur, Moira Shearer as Julia and Annette Page as Pepé, Julia's Dog

Photographs below by Anthony

THE QUEST: Archimago, a Magician

ADAM ZERO: The Mime, Adam Zero's spiritual adviser

DONALD OF THE BURTHENS: The King

Mandinian

COPPÉLIA: Dr. Coppelius

Anthony

MIRACLE IN THE GORBALS: A Beggar

MIRROR FOR WITCHES: Bilby

LES SIRÈNES: with Margot Fonteyn

Anthony

Baron

LE LAC DES CYGNES. *Above :* Margot Fonteyn as Odette, Leslie Edwards as Benno, Michael Somes as Prince Siegfried. *Below* (*left*) : Leslie Edwards as Benno, (*right*) as Master of Ceremonies

Paul Tanqueray

NOCTAMBULES : The Hypnotist

critic, said of this : ". . . a beautiful piece of work. Unlike most Coppeliuses, he is no semi-comic monster. He is an absent-minded poet, with a touch of Pierrot about him, moonstruck, idealistic, pre-destined to be the butt of fortune. Like a dedicated alchemist his whole being is concentrated on giving life to his masterpiece, the doll Coppélia. It is a completely original conception of the rôle, rich in possibilities, and bringing a wonderful color of fantasy to the ballet."

It will be seen that Mr. Edwards' career has not been one of spectacular success. He has been perhaps too unambitious, but the result of this has been that he plays a few secondary parts so well that they will always be associated with him.

Edwards has seen the Company grow from its small beginnings into a great national ballet company. Not a little of the present strength of the Company is derived from the steadfast devotion of dancers such as he, and Somes, Fonteyn and Farron. By their example they set the pace in many ways for the dancers of the Company, and ensure the continuity of the great traditions of the Company.

Hilarion in *Giselle* he was excellent and gave, and continues to give, a most carefully thought-out performance, gaining sympathy and pity for the unhappy gamekeeper whose love for Giselle is thwarted by Albrecht. Then came the weak and ailing king in *Donald of the Burthens*, followed by Bilby in *A Mirror for Witches*. As the foster-father of Doll, the daughter of a woman burned as a witch, he had a strong and sympathetic rôle, and in his scenes with his wife, a hard bitter woman (played magnificently by Julia Farron), and with Doll, he showed what a good dramatic actor he is.

In a new and lavish production of *Le Lac des Cygnes* in 1952 he was again Benno, and he also appeared in Act III as a Master of Ceremonies, directing the proceedings with the dignity of Cattalabutte. In *The Firebird* he was hardly recognisable as one of Kostchei's Attendants, and in Ashton's *Madame Chrysanthème* he made a brief appearance as a Dignitary. He was on the stage for only a few seconds, but he gave an amusing and authentic portrait of a Japanese official. In *Noctambules*, MacMillan's first ballet for the Sadler's Wells Ballet, he was the Hypnotist, around whom the whole action of the ballet revolves. In the early performances he seemed to lack the personal magnetism which such a character would have had, but he gave an impressive and dramatic performance, which continues to grow in strength and effect.

In this brief account of Leslie Edwards' career I have not mentioned all the parts he has played, but there are two which must be included : the name part in *Job*, where by his stillness he evokes the stoicism of this much tried man, and his Dr. Coppelius in *Coppélia*. John Martin, the eminent American

THE LADY AND THE FOOL : An Ambassador

Angus McBean

ROSEMARY LINDSAY

THE work of the Sadler's Wells School went on without a break during the War, in spite of innumerable difficulties. We have reason to be grateful for the fortitude and determination of the staff and students during those years, for a number of the leading soloists in the Company to-day were some of those war-time students. In 1943, for example, the senior students included Avril Navarre (who retired from the Company only recently), Philip Chatfield, Brian Earnshaw (now Shaw) and Rosemary Scott-Giles (now Lindsay). Miss Lindsay, who had been a student at the School since 1941, received her early training from Madame Anna Bromova, who had also been Leslie Edwards' teacher.

Rosemary Lindsay left the School in 1943, and became a member of the Company, making her début in *Casse-Noisette*. She was in the *corps de ballet* for several years, and when the Company moved to the Royal Opera House, Covent Garden, in 1946, at the first performance of *The Sleeping Beauty* on the 20th February, her name appeared among the village maidens, peasants, courtiers, heralds, etc., along with Pauline Wadsworth, Kenneth Melville, Brian Shaw and others. Not long after this she began to be noticed in various small parts : as one of the girls in red in *Les Patineurs*, as Estrella in *Carnaval*, and as one of the leaders of the swans in *Le Lac des Cygnes*. The following season she was a Child of Light in *Dante Sonata*, and appeared in *The Three-Cornered Hat* and *La Boutique Fantasque*. She first attracted the critics' notice towards the end of 1947, when she was one of the leading Wilis in *Giselle*. *The Dancing Times* noted that " special mention must be made of her short solo, in which she showed musicality and command of technique."

These two qualities, her sensibility and her assured technique, and her fair good looks and her natural intelligence, earned her a place the following year in *Symphonic Variations*. When the ballet was first performed in 1946, the three girls in it, Margot Fonteyn, Moira Shearer and Pamela May, seemed indispensable, but when Fonteyn was away in Paris, dancing with *Les Ballets des Champs-Élysées*, and a dancer had to be found to replace her, Rosemary Lindsay was chosen.

Symphonic Variations is a most lovely and rewarding work, but for the dancers it is a relentless and exacting ballet. The

John Hart

COPPÉLIA : Swanilda

dancers are on the stage all the time, and their response to the music must be perfect, their movements in perfect unison, their technique impeccable. Rosemary Lindsay's first performance lacked the clear-cut precision of May and Shearer, but it was a most creditable and promising performance, and when Shearer and May retired from the Company, Rosemary Lindsay became a regular member of the cast.

In 1952 she danced Aurora in *The Sleeping Beauty*. She approached the rôle with a gay determination and courage. The quality of her dancing was excellent, it was well phrased and she surmounted the difficulties of the Rose Adagio without undue strain. Her personality was perhaps too gentle and restrained for Aurora, but in her later performances it gained strength and added personality. As the Lilac Fairy in *The Sleeping Beauty* she gives one of her best performances. She has style and authority and a warm radiance, and she dances the difficult *variation* in the Prologue with great assurance and precision. Swanilda in *Coppélia*, which she first danced in 1953, is another leading rôle for which her natural gaiety and humour are well suited, but with a dozen other dancers in the Company available for the part, her opportunities to dance it have not been frequent.

Soon after Massine's ballet *Donald of the Burthens* was first produced, Beryl Grey, who danced the rôle of Death in it, was away with influenza, and at short notice Rosemary Lindsay took over the part. Her dancing was brilliant, she had force and vigour, and the evil aspect of the rôle was suitably emphasised.

Derek Allen

THE SLEEPING BEAUTY:
The Princess Aurora, Act I
Action photograph by Roger Wood
Left: in *GISELLE:* Queen of the Wilis
Below: left, in *SYMPHONIC VARIATIONS*
right, in *BALLET IMPERIAL*

Roger Wood

John Hart

ROSEMARY LINDSAY

THE SHADOW: A Young Girl, with (*left to right*) Brian Shaw, Desmond Doyle and Ronald Hynd as her Lovers

Action photograph by Paul Wilson

THE SHADOW: A Young Girl

Denis de Marney

Another rôle created by Beryl Grey was the black ballerina in *Ballet Imperial*, and this was also danced on many occasions by Rosemary Lindsay. It was not a part ideally suited to her, but she met its exacting technical demands with great ease and assurance, and she looked charming. In John Cranko's ballet *The Shadow*, produced in 1953, she created the part of the Young Girl and made a great success of it, although the extrovert young girl seemed far removed from the gentle personality she had displayed in other works.

She dances a wide range of parts in the current repertoire, and outstanding among them is her Queen of the Wilis in *Giselle*, a strong and vindictive character in her hands, and the Valse and the Prelude in *Les Sylphides*. In the Prelude, especially, one is aware of the lyric quality of her dancing and her ability to evoke the mood and feeling of the music. Then there is the Neapolitan Dance in *Le Lac des Cygnes*, and although she lacks Farron's special sparkle, she dances it with exciting speed and verve. *Façade* is not often included in the Sadler's Wells repertoire nowadays, but it was revived for the Twenty-fifth Birthday anniversary performance of the Company. On this occasion Rosemary Lindsay was chosen to dance the Polka. She danced it with great style, giving it a delicious subtlety and quiet humour. It made one wish there were other ballets in the repertoire which gave her similar opportunities to show her aptitude for comedy. The warmth of her reception after she had danced the Polka showed how much her performance was to the liking of the audience, and how much she has won their affection, as a loyal and hard working soloist, dancing every rôle that comes her way with the same freshness, intelligence and high technical achievement.

19

IN *LES SIRÈNES*

ALEXANDER GRANT

WHEN Alexander Grant jumped through a hoop at the first performance of Ashton's ballet *Les Sirènes* on 12th November 1946, a new and important male dancer was introduced to the public for the first time. Since that night he has created a score of important parts in new ballets, danced in many others and in the process, expended more vitality and energy than half a dozen other dancers put together.

He was born in Wellington, New Zealand, on 22nd February 1925, and he started dancing at the age of seven. His teachers were Kathleen O'Brien and Jeane Horne, and in his late teens he was awarded a scholarship, which is given in New Zealand by the Royal Academy of Dancing for dancers to study in London. He arrived in England on 1st February 1946, and was accepted by the Sadler's Wells School. Within a short time he was appearing, while still a student, with the Sadler's Wells Ballet at Covent Garden. He did not remain a student for long, and when the recently formed Sadler's Wells Theatre Ballet began giving performances, Grant joined the Company. On the 29th April 1946, he was in the Company's first performance of *Façade*, dancing the Popular Song with Donald Britton. A month later he created the part of the Old Man in Celia Franca's Persian ballet *Khadra*. The Company departed for its first tour a few weeks later, and after a fortnight, Grant was recalled to London to join the Sadler's Wells Ballet.

His early performances included the Youth in *Miracle in the Gorbals*, one of the four boys in *Les Patineurs* and a Grave-digger in *Hamlet*. He was in the Mazurka in *Coppélia*, the Czardas in *Le Lac des Cygnes* and a Cavalier in *The Sleeping Beauty*, in which he also appeared as one of the three Ivans.

His first important character part, in February 1947, was the Dandy in Massine's revival of his ballet *The Three-Cornered Hat*, in which he gave a neat little study. A few weeks later he was one of the dancing poodles in *La Boutique Fantasque*, and with his partner Pauline Clayden, made the most of an amusing little *pas de deux*.

In November 1947, came his first big opportunity. This was in Massine's new version of *Mam'zelle Angot*. The four leading parts were danced by Margot Fonteyn as Angot, Moira Shearer as the Aristocrat, Michael Somes as the Caricaturist and Alexander Grant as the Barber. In a tow-coloured wig he made the Barber an endearing and sympathetic little man. It was the kind of character Massine himself might have created. Grant's bounding vitality, his exceptional elevation, his comedy and his pathos made a strong impact on the audience, the Company and on Massine himself, and in Massine's next ballet for the Company, *The Clock Symphony*,

Edward Mandinicn

MAM'ZELLE ANGOT : As the Barber, with Margot Fonteyn in the title rôle

THE CLOCK SYMPHONY : The Clockmaker

FAÇADE : In the Tango as the Dago, with Nadia Nerina as the Debutante

Baron

Maurice Seymour

Roger Wood

CINDERELLA : The Jester

produced in June 1948, he again chose Grant for a leading rôle. In spite of the enchanting *décor* and costumes by Christian Bérard and the beauty of Moira Shearer as the Princess, the ballet was not a success. Young Grant, as the clockmaker on whom the Princess bestowed her favour, had little to work on in building up a character. It seemed then, as it does to-day, that Grant's true *forte* is in slightly grotesque characters. Like the Barber in *Mam'zelle Angot*, they must always be a little larger than life.

This was certainly true of his next creation : the Jester in Ashton's first full-length ballet *Cinderella*. Edwin Denby, the distinguished American critic, was delighted with the Jester's appearances, brief though they were. He praised the vitality and style of his performance, and expressed his belief that he " was the Company's most interesting male dancer." " Like a jet of fire," he wrote, " he darts forward in deep *plié*, in *renversé*, bent sideways, bent double, leaping down a flight of stairs, springing into the meagre dances of the guests with a smiling threat."

The Company's next new ballet was not until 20th February 1950, an unusually long interval due to the Company's absence abroad on its first American tour. The ballet was Ninette de Valois' *Don Quixote*, based on Cervantes' epic novel. Robert Helpmann was Don Quixote, Grant, Sancho Panza his servant and friend, and Margot Fonteyn danced the dual rôle of the Lady Dulcinea and Aldonza Lorenzo. Grant's Sancho Panza was brilliantly conceived. He made him a real, believable character, greasy, uncouth and faithful after his fashion to his noble master. A few months later came another

Left above : DAPHNIS AND CHLOÉ : As Bryaxis, a Pirate Chief, with Margot Fonteyn as Chloé, a Shepherdess   *Action photograph by Roger Wood*

Left below : BALLABILE : With Anne Negus   *Baron*

Roger Wood

DON QUIXOTE: Sancho Panza

creation of a quite different order. In Roland
Petit's *Ballabile*, Violetta Elvin and Grant had
the leading parts in a series of richly inventive
scenes. Of Grant's many amusing moments in
this light-hearted work, one remembers best his
ludicrous appearance in a long black coat, a
bowler hat and an umbrella, but his amazing
vitality and his broad sense of humour made his
presence felt throughout the ballet. Without him
it would have been very thin beer, and even
Grant had to work very hard to make the
sustained joke amusing. His next important
creation was as Bryaxis, a Pirate Chief in Ashton's

Tiresias, a vigorous and villainous looking character. Then came another major part in *Donald
of the Burthens*, a new ballet by Massine with a
Scottish setting. The ballet had a scenario which
it was quite impossible to convey in terms of
ballet, and in spite of the efforts of Beryl Grey
as Death and Grant as Donald, the ballet was a
failure. Although Grant excels in the quick
angular style of Massine's character parts, this
part had too little real substance in it for a
complete or even an interesting character, and it
was not Grant's fault that the character of Donald
never really emerged.

ALEXANDER
GRANT

DONALD OF THE BURTHENS: As Donald with Beryl Grey as
Death in the first scene of the ballet

Baron

BONNE BOUCHE: As the
Black King

Anthony

Anthony

THE RAKE'S PROGRESS : As The Rake

Felix Fonteyn

SYLVIA : Margot Fonteyn as Sylvia, John Hart as Orion
and Alexander Grant as Eros

THE THREE-CORNERED HAT : As The Miller

Angus McBean

SCÈNES DE BALLET : With Nadia Nerina

Photograph by Roger Wood

25

LE LAC DES CYGNES : In the Neapolitan
Dance   *Houston Rogers*

His next new part was the Black King in John
Cranko's burlesque ballet *Bonne Bouche,* and in a
flamboyant uniform, he had a riotous time in
South Kensington and in his native Africa. After
Cranko's cautionary tale, as he called it, came
Sylvia, Ashton's second full-length ballet. In
this Grant appeared as the God Eros. He was
unbelievably static for most of the first act,
standing so motionless that most of the audience
imagined he was a statue. When he came to
life he was a pleasant mixture of strength and
trickery, although the part made no great demands on his powers of characterisation.

In a new production of *Le Lac des Cygnes* in
1952, Ashton arranged a Neapolitan Dance for
Act III, which gave Grant and Farron a magnificent opportunity to display their speed and
vitality. Ashton also created an elegant *pas de
six* for Act I, in which Grant as the leading boy
danced with great style and *élan.* With Rosemary
Lindsay as his partner, he led the young lovers
in Andrée Howard's *Veneziana,* and in the
Coronation ballet in 1953, *Homage to the Queen,*
he had a spectacular solo as the Spirit of Fire.
In Ashton's next new ballet for the Company,
Variations on a Theme of Purcell, in January 1955,

MADAME CHRYSANTHÈME : With Elaine
Fifieldas Mme. Chrysanthème and Alexander Grant
as Pierre, a French sailor.

Right-hand page :
MADAME CHRYSANTHÈME : Elaine Fifield
and Alexander Grant   *Baron*

Grant was the central character. Half-faun,
half-jester and in a variety of costumes, he
expended a great deal of energy to little purpose,
and in contrast to the cold elegance of the other
dancers he seemed brash and a little vulgar. His
next new rôle was as Pierre, a French sailor, in
Ashton's *Madame Chrysanthème.* His Pierre was a
likeable character, and although perhaps he made
him look more like a British than a French sailor,
he was completely convincing and danced
brilliantly.

In *Birthday Offering,* Ashton's *pièce d'occasion* to
celebrate the Company's Twenty-fifth Birthday,
he partnered Nadia Nerina, and with the six
other men in the ballet, demonstrated as never
before that our National Ballet has produced
some magnificent male dancers.

Grant dances many other parts in the repertoire : Franz in *Coppélia,* Satan in *Job,* in which
he is a worthy successor to his great predecessors
in the part, Helpmann and Dolin, the rôle
created by Somes in *Scènes de Ballet,* the leading
Ivan in the Three Ivans in *The Sleeping Beauty,*
the Dago in *Façade,* the Rake in *The Rake's
Progress* and the Miller in *The Three-Cornered Hat,*
in which he gives a performance which is far
removed from the choreographer's performance
in the part. It is unusual to complain of a
dancer's excess of vitality, but on rare occasions
Grant over-plays, over-dances and throws re-
straint overboard. But all in all, what a magnificent dancer he is, and what a remarkable
record of achievement he has attained at only
mid-way in his career.

Anthony

TRITSCH-TRATSCH: Elaine Fifield as the Girl

LE LAC DES CYGNES: As Odette

Anthony

Anthony

PINEAPPLE POLL: Elaine Fifield as Pineapple Poll

ELAINE FIFIELD

WHEN Frederick Ashton created his *Birthday Offering* for the Twenty-fifth Anniversary performance of the Sadler's Wells Ballet he included Elaine Fifield as one of his seven ballerinas. Although at that time her ranking in the Company was that of soloist, it was a certain indication that her promotion would not be long delayed, and she was in fact appointed ballerina in August 1956.

She is an exquisite dancer. She dances with her whole body, and there seems to be nothing that she cannot do, so far as dancing is concerned. What she lacks at present is the ability to project character in so large a theatre as the Royal Opera House, but after a slow start and with some uncertainty at times, she is learning to express the emotional aspects of the great rôles in classical ballet : Aurora in *The Sleeping Beauty* and Odette–Odile in *Le Lac des Cygnes*, and both these parts she now dances with growing assurance.

All that I can do in the short space available is to give a brief record of Miss Fifield's career to date, and reserve a more detailed account for a volume devoted entirely to her work.

Elaine Fifield was born in Sydney on 28th October 1930. She studied dancing at the Frances Scully School, Sydney, and in 1945 she was awarded a scholarship to enable her to come to England for further training. She joined the Sadler's Wells School in September 1946, and less than a year later, in August 1947, became

REFLECTION: As Echo in John Cranko's
ballet for the Sadler's Wells Theatre Ballet
Denis de Marney

a member of the Sadler's Wells Theatre Ballet.
By the autumn of 1948 she had become a leading
dancer in the Company, and remained in this
position until 1954 when she joined the Sadler's
Wells Ballet.

In a company of talented youngsters, Elaine
Fifield stood out. She was both a classicist and
a *demi-caractère* dancer, and there was a special
quality about her dancing and her personality
which attracted the attention of choreographers
—the highest tribute a dancer can receive.

The first part created for her was in John
Cranko's little trio *Tritsch-Tratsch*, in September
1947. Then came a part in Ashton's *Valses Nobles
and Sentimentales*, followed by the leading girl's
part in Antony Burke's plotless work *Parures*. In
November 1948 she had the name part in Andrée
Howard's *Selina*, and in March 1950 in Somes'
ballet *Summer Interlude*, she and David Blair were
the principal bathers. She had a secondary rôle
in Balanchine's ballet *Trumpet Concerto*, but in
John Cranko's *Pastorale* which was first produced
in 1950, as Diaphenia she had an important part
which earned high praise for the lovely, easy
grace of her performance. One of her finest
creations was the title rôle in Cranko's *Pineapple
Poll*. As Echo in *Reflection*, a symbolic and
abstract ballet, she gave a hauntingly beautiful
performance, and a month later in September
1952, she was the principal Siren in Rodrigues'
ballet *Île des Sirènes*. In Rodrigues' next ballet,
Blood Wedding, in June 1953, she had a passionate
and dramatic rôle as the Bride.

During the Company's first American tour in
1951-52, Miss Fifield married John Lanchbery,
the musical director of the Company, and a
daughter, born 13th April 1954, necessitated Miss
Fifield's absence from the Company during the
season 1953-54. On her return to dancing Miss
Fifield moved to the Sadler's Wells Ballet, making
her first appearance with the Company in
October 1954, in the *pas de six* in *Le Lac des
Cygnes*. She danced her first Swanilda with the
Company on 22nd January 1955. A few months
later, on 1st April 1955, she created her first part
in the Company, the title-rôle in Ashton's *Madame
Chrysanthème*, and although her personality was
a little too small for the vast theatre, the pure
beauty of her dancing won her an enthusiastic
reception. Ill health prevented her from accom-
panying the Company to America for their fourth
tour, but she revisited the Theatre Ballet with
great success. In the Twenty-fifth Birthday
Season, she danced for the first time Aurora in
The Sleeping Beauty, and Odette–Odile in *Le Lac
des Cygnes*. She appeared in Ashton's *Birthday
Offering*, and prepared for her third creation for
the Company, in Rodrigues' *The Miraculous
Mandarin*, first presented at the Edinburgh
Festival in August 1956.

THE SLEEPING BEAUTY : Elaine Fifield as the Princess Aurora, David Blair as Prince Florimund

DAVID BLAIR

THE wealth of talent in the Sadler's Wells Ballet to-day is due, in no small measure, to the dancers who received their early stage experience with the sister company, the Sadler's Wells Theatre Ballet. Outstanding among these is David Blair, and if all goes well with his subsequent career and success does not spoil him, he may well become one of the outstanding male dancers of his generation in the world to-day.

The son of John and Zetté Butterfield, Blair

DAVID BLAIR

was born in 1932. He began dancing lessons at the age of eight at Madame Amy Ibbetson's school in Halifax. Here he was given an excellent groundwork in technique, taught to work hard, and encouraged to persevere. In 1946 Mme. Ibbetson took him to Sadler's Wells for an audition. He was accepted immediately and granted a scholarship which was more generous than any previously granted, and provided for all his needs during the eighteen months he was at the school. The one fear was that he would not grow tall enough to be a dancer. He joined the Sadler's Wells Theatre Ballet towards the end of 1947, and although he was still too short in stature to be a member of the *corps de ballet*, parts were found for him, and when the Company visited his native town in December 1947, he danced the Younger Brother in Alan Carter's *The Catch*.

He began to grow a little, and to take an increasingly active part in the ballets in the repertoire and in new productions, and by the autumn of 1949 audiences and critics alike began to realise that young Blair might have a considerable future. At one *matinée* in October 1949, Richard Buckle saw him dance, and wrote in his magazine *Ballet*:

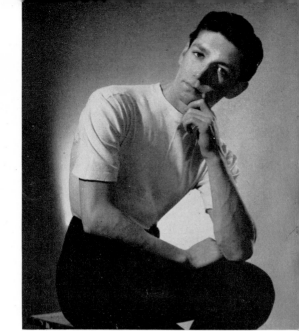

Anthony

DAVID BLAIR in practice costume

Baron

PASTORALE

Anthony

PINEAPPLE POLL: As Captain Belaye
of *H.M.S. Hot Cross Bun*

DAVID BLAIR

Top : In *LES SYLPHIDES*

Below : GISELLE : With Violetta Elvin

Photographs by Baron

" This . . . young man, who to-day danced the Burgmuller *pas de deux* from *Giselle*, with the vivacious and agile Maryon Lane, is only seventeen ; he has a fine carriage, handsome appearance, good proportions, pleasing stage personality, good feet, and no mean technique. We shall see what happens to him."

Briefly, what has happened to him is this : he became the leading male dancer of the Company, creating a number of important parts in Cranko's ballets, (including Damon in *Pastorale*, Captain Belaye in *Pineapple Poll*, and Harlequin in *Harlequin in April*), and in Rodrigues' *Île des Sirènes*. He danced Franz in *Coppélia*, and the Prince in *Casse-Noisette*, and appeared in many of the other ballets in the repertoire. Anton Dolin, impressed by his promise, coached him in the difficult art of *pas de deux*. He received extra instruction from Vera Volkova and Audrey De Vos, and above all he received the regular encouragement and attention of Ninette de Valois, and daily coaching and instruction from Peggy van Praagh. Blair worked increasingly hard, justifying the faith placed in him by his teachers.

It was inevitable that he would join the Sadler's Wells Ballet, and he became a member of the Company in the summer of 1953. It took him a little time to get used to his new surroundings and his relatively minor position in the Company, but he made steady progress and in time he began to dance leading rôles, such as the Red Knight in *Checkmate* and the Caricaturist in *Mam'zelle Angot*. But the full potentiality of his range as a dancer was not seen until the Twenty-fifth Anniversary Season of 1956, when he danced within a few months the leading male rôles in *The Sleeping Beauty*, *Le Lac des Cygnes*, *Giselle* and Ashton's *Cinderella*. Here indeed was a true *danseur noble* : an excellent partner, a superb executant in his own *variations*, with a pleasing presence, and a personality which filled the vast theatre. To make such a satisfactory début in the great male rôles of classical ballet was a happy augury for his future development as a dancer. Obviously there was still room for development, but no one, one felt, was more conscious of this than Mr. Blair, and he made great progress in all these rôles before the end of the season. He was one of the seven male dancers in Ashton's *Birthday Offering*, and in the last few weeks of the season prepared for the principal male part in Cranko's first full-length ballet, *The Prince of the Pagodas*.